Praise for *The Book of ...*

I love this book. Never t ... the
ways nondisabled wome ... ier.
Davio's range is exquisit ... _ ... poetic tradition —
ballad, litany, pantoum — while making room in poetry for disabled
femmes, funny as hell, and powerful.

— Jillian Weise

Davio's *Unreal Woman* is a meditation on sickness and shortcoming
and sorrow, and yet is not so simply summed. The Unreal Woman
rises and falls — metaphorically and literally — at the hands of a
world refusing to see her. Isolated by blame, cures for weakness are
hurled from behind department store displays, walls of yoga mats,
and the safety of social media medical degrees. The Unreal Woman
takes the question "Why can't you just...?" and turns it inside out.

— Camille Griep

The Unreal Woman is like "The palm at the end of the mind"— that
Stevensian trick for we both see her and do not. These are poems
of spirit and embodiment; of appearance and disappearance. This
collection brings forward the shy, unasked for recognitions and
ironies of our tragicomic predicament.

— Stephen Kuusisto

Also by Kelly Davio

It's Just Nerves: Notes on a Disability	(Squares & Rebels, 2017)
Burn This House	(Red Hen Press, 2013)

THE BOOK OF THE UNREAL WOMAN

Kelly Davio

ISBN: 978-1-915079-89-3

Cover designed by Aaron Kent

Edited and typeset by Aaron Kent

Broken Sleep Books Ltd
Rhydwen,
Talgarreg,
SA44 4HB
Wales

Contents

Real Women   11

The Unreal Woman is a Bad Person   13

The Unreal Woman's Imperfections   14

The Unreal Woman has Salman Rushdie's Dreamy Eyes   16

The Unreal Woman at the Grocery   17

Fainting in Public Toilets, According to the Unreal Woman   19

Instructions for Unreal Women: For Best Results   21

The Unreal Woman Isn't Ordering Steak   24

The Unreal Woman Asks You to Put Her Suitcase in [...]   25

Dear Body,   29

He Died After a Long Illness   32

A Normal Life   33

June is Myasthenia Gravis Awareness Month   35

Tell the Action Film Heroine Her Life is in Danger   36

The Man Who Punched Me in Seattle   37

Pantoum for Someone Else's Child   39

At the Minneapolis Children's Museum,   40

On Gravity   42

I May Appear Drunk   47

In the Infusion Center,   49

"In The Kingdom of Thud, Globes Plummet to Black"   50

Immunosuppressive Therapy: I (a praise song)   51

Immunosuppressive Therapy II (a litany)   53

Immunosuppressive Therapy: III (a prayer)   55

"Doctors baffled about why H1N1 targets young, healthy"   57

Immunosuppressive Therapy: IV (as suspense film)   58

Round for Corticosteroids   61

Intravenous Immunoglobulin Therapy: I   62

Intravenous Immunoglobulin Therapy: II   64

Etymological Note   66

The Unreal Woman, Post-Operative   71

Acknowledgements   81

You didn't know I had a DREAD DISEASE didja? Well I got one.
— Flannery O'Connor, *The Habit of Being*

The Book of the Unreal Woman

Kelly Davio

for Elizabeth Hess

I.
The Unreal Woman

Real Women
— *"Real Women Have Curves"*

They fit in XL tights, we're told.
Their volume fills the special-order bras
built wide enough about the lacey bands
to suggest a well formed plentitude

in fully lined and double-lettered cups.
Real women give birth to multitudes
of Gerber-blonde babies in a continual
swell and retraction not unlike that

of a latex balloon, so quick to snap back
to size. Real women, after all, work out.
They repeat a mantra: *healthy is the new*,
but forget what was *old*. They raise dumbbells

and celebrate themselves. They know
what would fix you, Unreal Woman, disposing
of your sharps in the bright orange canister.
They have tut-tutted you, Unreal Woman,

when bottled prescriptions spill forth
from your open purse. They have watched you,
Unreal Woman, vertiginous and clutching
for the staircase handrail or shuffle-stepping

with a limp, your slacks dangling from meatless
hips, from bony kneecaps. And under the Lasik
clarity of their vision, Unreal Woman, you
become small as they expand, claim the space

you were never meant to occupy. They start
with your hair, thinning from steroids,
and thread it out by the root. They nibble
at the keratin of your fingernails, roll skin

from your limbs like wet paper, knock
your bones together in a jaunty tune.
Seconds are all it takes to absorb you.
Real women, they eat your heart out.

The Unreal Woman is a Bad Person

and she knows it. When the staring child in the market asks what's happened to her, she replies, *the same thing that's going to happen to you someday,* and finds herself amusing. She takes up too much space—claims public territory like a small country unto herself, this bus bench her personal kingdom, this sidewalk her one-woman lane. When a man behind her sighs at her slow lumber down the pavement, she invents elaborate scenarios of just what he might do with himself, a sharp object, and a little spare time. She lets the rubber tip of her cane wear through, allows it to clack with a tin-can ring on the floors of the bank, the mall, pharmacy. Every grating metal rattle says *I am here, I am here, I am here.*

The Unreal Woman's Imperfections

Houses and rooms are full of perfumes...
I breathe the fragrance myself and know it and like it.
— Walt Whitman

This steroidal flush of prednisolone
is the closest the Unreal Woman will come
to a second adolescence: the impressive
constellation of acne rises from the deep

and interstellar spaces of her pores,
looms up through the layers of skin
like a slow and aching supernova. She buys
a copy of *Teen Vogue,* scans for tips on breakouts,

finds articles on breakups. The Unreal Woman
wanders the makeup megamart, the skincare
city, sorts through pots and jars of unction,
cakes and slabs that promise to hide any woman's

imperfections. Each heavy resurfacer will,
she is told in labels and back-of-bottle
copy, look natural. She picks out a *primer*
as though her face were a pocked sheet

of drywall, the lines of her increasing age
collateral damage in a slapdash plaster job.
She rubs a test glob over pale wrists
before turning her attention to *foundation,*

that weighty brick-and-mortar. It promises
her scars will fade, and her lumpy skin appear
smooth like a ripe and sun-warmed peach.
She globs a swatch of pigment on her chin,

watches its pink undertones turn her the shade
of a cartoon piglet: sweaty and downed with hair
that pops in high relief on skin rollicked
with pits and lumps of healing tissue.

The Unreal Woman is inspired. She grabs
a mango lip balm, uses a clean swab to orange it
across her mouth and make a garish X to draw
the gaze from spots. She poofs a cloud of bronzer

over her chipmunk-swelling cheeks, allows
dark pigment to settle into wrinkles, to simulate
a hollow, a false structure of bone. She inspects
her profile with a sidelong glance in the mirror.

She approves of herself, and fills her nose
with the in-breath of talc. She exhales, and a cloud
of rouge lifts her. She rises over the linoleum floor,
her soul glittering in the overhead light.

The Unreal Woman has Salman Rushdie's Dreamy Eyes

They droop—do you see? Levator muscles grow tired,
too weak to hold the lids in place. The forehead smoothes
and brows slip as though dangling a garment loose

in a striptease, a fan dance of lashes. A flash of pupil
and a half-revealed iris are the bedroomiest of all, at least
on famous men. But somehow, ptosis looks less charming

on her. Her face buckles, folding the liner she's flicked
into a perfect cat's eye. Her cheeks can't hold
the weight of dark circles—subcutaneous fat laps

onto cheekbones. By her own assessment, the Unreal Woman
resembles no one so much as Phineas Gage after TNT
drove an iron rod through his gourd, his melon,

his miraculous skull. The only marvel the Unreal Woman
ascribes to her own cranial structure is that her nose,
that knobby crag, protuberant ledge, can still hold a pair

of outsized sunglasses. Think of Coco Chanel's metastatic
frames, white saucers that block both sun and the gaping
of strangers. Behind the lens, she is a mystery. She is a star.

The Unreal Woman at the Grocery

"What price bananas? Are you my Angel?"
— Alan Ginsberg

Her cart is mighty, for she piles it
with the semblance of health: fruit
that shines in the overhead fluorescents

with a fat coating of wax, vegetables
in cruciform, their closed buds rising
like small antennae from stalks.

She drives that cart like serfs dragged
monoliths into henges, scuffing the soil
as they went. She heaves the bags of plain

the cans of saltless, the boxes of expeller-
pressed tasteless into the cart, and it rings
with each drop of bulk. She coasts aisles,

bent at the waist to heave the rolling heap,
and from the way she slaloms past babies
waddling gummy-handed through the beans,

from the way she keeps momentum
past the aproned men who ask her
if she's finding all she needs. She is not,

yet she rolls on. Her fixed mouth gives her
the look of knowing as she shuffles behind
the juggernaut. Perhaps the look in her eye,

the look that suggests the entire apparatus
might slip from control at any moment,
is why strangers stop her, ask her questions

she's unprepared to answer. Perhaps
they want to watch as the cart's wheels
roll away from her while they pepper

her with needs: *where's the clam chowder?*
What's the best way to get urine out
of a couch? She doesn't know, and she

doesn't know. Please understand: she doesn't
work here. It takes her aisles and then some
to get her momentum back.

Fainting in Public Toilets, According to the Unreal Woman

When the blackout shine sweeps a pall
across her vision, it sparkles with dark stars
as the Unreal Woman's skin glistens in a cold

shimmer of sweat. The outrushing blood
drums vitreous in her eye,
as an erratic heartbeat wallops her ribcage.

To find a restroom quickly—that's the trick.
Hallways form gauntlets of out-swinging doors,
and department store floors, so spiny

with high-heeled shoes, aren't safe at all.
Sidewalks aren't worth consideration, because
nothing says *drunk* like an arms-out loll

in scuttle of crunched leaf and newsprint.
No, the disabled stall in the ladies' loo
is best. Latch the door and there's privacy

enough for fainting. The Unreal Woman knows
by now how to creep to the floor, flatten the spine
flush with the ripple of tile. She's learned

to prop the feet above the heart, her socks
white flags to the universe. She laces fingers
across her abdomen, lets shanks of sweaty hair

weave their drippy way into the floor's grout.
If the spider behind the toilet makes it way
across the tile to inspect her with one probing leg,

she will welcome his quiet company, his lack
of comment as he watches her go. Her consciousness
spins out and away, weblike at the ceiling.

Instructions for Unreal Women: For Best Results

After surgery, you may experience
            unintended weight loss.
            Pretend to be grateful
            about this fact. Loose-
            fitting clothing will help
            to cover the protrusion
            of your hipbones, your ribs.
            Long hair allowed to fall
            across your hollowed cheeks
            forms an excellent mask.

It is important that you remain active
            during your recovery.
            Remember that activity
            has an alarming way
            of further reducing both you
            and the space you occupy.
            Pretend to be grateful
            about this fact, too.

Try to maintain your social life.
            Understand that acquaintances
            will congratulate you
            for the loss of the wobble
            you never understood
            to be unsightly. It's best
            to nod in this case, and turn
            your chatter to any range
            of current events. If caught

unequipped, you may turn to facts
you learned from nature programs
while propped in a pneumatic
hospital bed.

Understand that you may experience
one variation of response:
the hand-on-the-shoulder
suggestion of disordered eating.
Your protruding bone blade
will do little to discourage
this line of inquiry. You may,
despite inadequate musculature
in your throat and the vile
churn of your stomach,
be tempted to make
a public display of eating.

If, against your better judgment,
you choose to consume
a foodstuff in front of your
inquisitor, make a wise
selection. That raw carrot
will only gag you and entrench
her suspicions. If you reach
for the cube of cheese, soft
enough to slide down the throat
without incident, she'll say
I wish I could eat like you
and compliment your metabolic
speed. It is best to express
your gratitude once more.

For best results, avoid strong sunlight,
as exposure increases your risk
of being seen. If you must
go out in daylight hours,
position yourself to cast
a substantial shadow.
Give the illusion of substance.

The Unreal Woman Isn't Ordering Steak

Her ambitions aren't that high, and besides,
she never cared all that much for sinew.
But after years of boiled, of bland, of soft,
you don't want to know what she'd do
for a wedge of crispy iceberg or a thick
wheel of carrot. A scalloped cucumber
with waxy skin would send her into fits
of glee; she has lengthy fantasies starring
escarole. But breaking through the fiber
would require mastication, and the firing
of muscle fiber itself would want for the pop
of neurotransmission, for the hiss and fizz
in each receptor and as it fired to life: too
many variables, each one over-determined
to fail. She sips water to dull her hunger.
She'll just have a coffee, thanks. Coughs
to cover the rumble of her stomach,
douses her mug with cream to stave off
the coming blood-sugar crash, the temple-
throbbing headache. No, she's *not
hungry*. She repeats it until it feels true.

The Unreal Woman Asks You to Put Her Suitcase in the Overhead Compartment

You let her struggle with it a moment,
watch her lift the hardshell case
like an offering to some low god,
arms trembling in awe of the divine.

You round your shoulders, tuck
your elbows in, so appropriately,
counting seconds while she blocks
the flow of business suits in the aisle.

You could be seated by now, downing
a bloody mary if not for her sweaty
ministry of the suitcase, threatening
to knock that old lady in the head

with a slip of her hand. You wait
until she asks you, turns her face up
as she says *I'm sorry, could you?*
She knows it's not your job to lift

what she's freely chose to pack.
There are people paid to do this,
but they're not going to help.
Because they are busy rattling ice

in the forward galley. Because
they're securing the cabin. Because
that's what travel's come to. *You*
ought to charge a fee for handling bags.

You ought to make this woman buy you
that cocktail. You tell her this, all of it,
as you toss her case, feather light,
into the compartment and snap its latch

with a plastic twang. You settle back
into your seat and clasp the buckle,
low and tight, around your abundant
midsection. You are what is right

in America today. You deserve more
than her *thank you*. What about
an upgrade? You turn to the woman
and ask about that drink.

II.
Dear Body

Dear Body,

—after Philip Memmer

Forgive me: before this message, I've tried
        to reach you though the customary channels.
                I dropped a line to your business address,

                then later, with some qualms over manners,
        your personal email, the one at which
I imagine, your close friends send chain mail.

I have a few requests; I wanted to bend
        our mutual ear, and thought it best to deal
                with our joint interests directly, to cease

                miscommunication through scraps of data,
        through lab reports generated by the hospital's
automated systems. Let's be honest: do either of us

know what to make of the milk-ghost images
        shot through with X-rays? Yet having heard
                no reply after what I myself would characterize

                as a civil interval, I confess that I tried
        calling you. Perhaps you were out—you let
the line ring for some minutes, no machine

catching the call. I wondered, briefly,
        whether you knew it was me on the wire,
                whether you read our name on a pop-up screen

                and decided to wait me out. But speculation
        is beside the point. I trust that you can appreciate
my position: after decades of working together

toward what I believe is our common good,
        I've been surprised by your recent failures
                of good faith. I hope I do not go too far, but

                I view your recalcitrance as willful disregard.
        When I desire to grasp, say, an apple—does it matter
why?—I feel I can expect your help, your closing

of fingers around the green rind. Or when I need
        the knee to hold, the joint to bend appropriately,
                that I shouldn't need to wonder if you'll comply

                or toss me to the ground. You've left me,
        I confess, in a spasm that looks for all the world
like a drunk's bungling rage. I've tried

to appease or inspire you, shouting down
        the nerve-trip wires with pill after dissolving
                pill, but you don't seem cheered. I've considered

                the possible dissolution of our partnership,
        but on further reflection, I do not see a viable
alternative to our continued work together.

I hope I do not seem too familiar, too cavalier
        if I say that I have grown to like you, over time.
                At the outset of our working relationship, I may

                have thought you a bit ungainly, and might've made
        some remarks uncomplimentary to your appearance.
For these, I am sorry: I see now that the texture

of your hair or the general curvature of your muscle
        and fat is in no way my concern, for you are
                an independent entity. I hope that any dismissive

                comments on my part are not to blame for our current
        state of affairs, and that we may repair the rapport
we once took as a given. Please, consider

replying to this letter. Whether by post or email
        is at your discretion. In case you choose to call,
                I'll be waiting with our hand on the phone.

He Died After a Long Illness

That's how the obituaries phrase it. He had
an *underlying condition,* they assure us.
We shake the newspaper free of its creases
and are comforted, somehow, by the conditions
of death. We are invited to imagine it as a pebble,
flung by chance or wedged by a bystander
into the long-grinding gears of pain. A mercy,
we say to one another. A kindness, really.
We assure ourselves that nothing underlies us;
no pathogenic beasts rumble under mattresses
while we lie open-eyed in the dark, unable to sleep
for the shadows that loom on our walls. We
don't need mercy. We laugh at kindness.
Our gears rotate freely on, greased by luck,
by good and careful programming of genes.

A Normal Life

My friend bakes cherry pie each time
her football team comes flickering
across the holy blue light of the screen

which is weekly. I do not mind,
for I eat the pie, and in case of victory
we bless the crust, praise the efficacy

of suet and flour. In the case of a rout,
which is often, we blame humidity
or atmospheric pressure for deflating

the tender flake of dough. We pretend
this kitchen experiment—with its loose relation
to a playoff win several years ago—

is a causal relation for all of time and sport.
Forking our slices, ladling Dream Whip,
we eat. We grow round and are sated.

*

She asks me why I *do it to myself*,
this daily ingestion of steroid that slicks
my face with sweat and oil, daubing be damned,

and makes a rogue swell of my belly.
My stomach plumps with water in the manner
of brined chicken, and she wants to know

why I can't try a bit of yoga, maybe jogging.
She's read articles in women's mags, seen ads
on the internet. Don't I get tired, she wants

to know, of putting myself through it?
Of sinking my stock into rattling pills
that don't let me lead *a normal life*? I smile,

swipe a forkful of pie crust through the neon
pink of syrup. A man barrels his padded body
into another's on a frozen field. I eat and am filled.

June is Myasthenia Gravis Awareness Month

It's been waiting all this inanimate time.
A bilge of antibodies swamping the blood,
its proteins have latched themselves to nerves
and hung like barely breathing suckerfish
for centuries. But just as the primordial bisque
gave rise to a stew of organic flesh, the disease
is ready for its heyday, it's evolutionary shot
at the bigtime. The transformation starts at the 5k
run, the fundraiser with its pancake breakfast
to follow. The antibodies suck in the juice
from the electric blue of the awareness ribbons,
jolt down the safety pins lodged in running bibs.
They gather nerve from boomboxes that treble along
to *I Will Survive* at water stations. The proteins clot,
knock together with each footfall on asphalt,
gather the first jolts of sentience. Hungry, they stalk
the sneakered masses and prepare for the onslaught,
ready to collapse each hard-running pair of legs
in a zombie-flapping jig. Its consciousness fires
the first rounds in the evolutionary chamber.

Tell the Action Film Heroine Her Life is in Danger

and she'll scoff, chin leveled at the horizon.
Enemy choppers will thwack their outlines
against a backdrop of pyramids and ancient dust,
and our heroine will spit, no less to clear grit from teeth

than to show she's taking it like a real man, this meaningless
threat to life. Why live, after all, if she can't stomp her way
across the world's deserts in heavy-soled boots
and jeans distressed in just the right places?

Maybe if the consulting surgeon threw open the door,
preemptively armed with scalpel and bone saw,
I could be so brave as to turn my head and spit
on this Lysol-reeking floor. If the anesthesiologist

brandished a rag soaked in ether. If nurses descended
by elaborate belay system from behind the acoustical tiles,
dropping a makeshift theatre of surgery right here,
right now. Maybe then I wouldn't ask the surgeon to hear—

one more time—the percentage-worth of chance that,
while he carves away at my chest with his archeological kit,
my heart, far from stoic, could go still without the benefit
of an orchestral swell in the soundtrack, dead without applause.

The Man Who Punched Me in Seattle

Wore a red sweatshirt that made his fists
look like a child's, poking out as they did
from Hanes ribbed cuffs. Hardly the kind

to make a woman reach for her pepper spray:
no incoherent ranting, no sneaky grope in a hall.
Just a stubbled man, at middle age, with nowhere

better to be. As the cushioned tip of my cane
sucked itself to concrete in my shuffle-step walk,
he waited until I'd stepped just past him

to wind back his arm and land a knuckled lob
at my shoulder. What syllable escaped me
when my hand turned loose my purse

and the contents of my bags scattered free,
my arms flapping *hello-goodbye* for balance?
And did it harmonize with the crack

of my kneecaps on the ground, first one,
then its bony other, with the aluminum ring
of my adjustable cane jingling like flung coins?

It must not have been what he'd imagined,
the unseemly stretch of slacks in a crouch,
my jacket scrunching up under the arms,

the messy rumple of hair flapped forward.
He shook his head, a wet chuckle bubbling
on his lips. "I wasn't trying to hit somebody

with a cane," he said not to me.
Head cocked like a pigeon's,
he waited, as though for apology. "That,"

he said, jabbing a finger at the tangle
of limbs before him, my arm stretched for the cane
beyond my reach, "That is just my luck."

Pantoum for Someone Else's Child

Biology tells me I should want this:
a chubby infant, cannonball snug as he naps
on my belly, we two a faintly breathing heap
as his mother lists, arms freed for a moment.

My friend's baby, chubby cannonball that naps
in my lap, doesn't care that he's not my son,
that I'll leave this house with my arms free
of his milk-fed weight, none of my genes his.

He's not my child, but evolution doesn't care,
says *wouldn't this be nice?* Forgets my hazards,
these faulty genes of mine that could be his,
the lurking danger that spins in my DNA.

Wouldn't this be nice? Evolution says. Forget
that one chance in five of death on arrival.
Ignore the lurking codes that twist my DNA,
that would unwind the springs of his legs.

That one-in-five chance: worse odds
than one bullet in a crank of empty chambers.
I unwind his legs that go springing at my ribs
while his feet punch me from the outside in.

Evolution abhors an empty chamber, scoffs
at the image of a faintly breathing heap
in an incubator. Biology kicks me
from the outside in, tells me I should want this.

At the Minneapolis Children's Museum,

We speak Spanish. Thankfully, you
are only two years old. With three years
of classes on my high school transcripts,

though decades buffer then and now,
you and I reach basic understandings.
I ask for your *mano,* and you hold mine.

You suggest a brisk removal of shoes,
and I give you the bilingual *no.* I wonder
whether I might have reviewed a few verbs

on the way to your house, one or two nouns
for basic objects on the plane-ride east.
As mothers waddle their children inside

from the endless crunch of salted snow,
they smile at me while their toddlers charge,
toes stubbing the juice-stained carpet.

I wonder what they make of the woman
asking you, in butchered phrasing, to identify
azul, verde, and *rojo,* smiling, if diffident,

as you sticky-slap your palms on blocks.
I'm relieved that you're understanding
with your parents' pasty friend, patient

as you shuffle to show me your favorite
push-buttons, to demonstrate the operation
of all the best whirligigs. You're so sure of me,

certain that I know where to find the cheerios
in the diaper bag, that I have full access
to your sippy cup, that I possess the power

to keep the older kids from splashing water
on your jumper as you when you dip a little boat
into a chlorinated, inch-deep tub.

I suspect you know, somehow, that *titi*
would have no idea what to do or say
if you suddenly began to cry, if you decided

you'd rather wail for you mother, cry
for your spaniel or demand that your father
give you a slice of bread from the special shop

across the city. I proffer you a Tupperware
teeming with goldfish crackers. We nod to one another,
neither of us much good at conversation.

On Gravity

I.

A census of objects I have dropped:
>   knives, blade down and wiggling into floors,

unsheathed markers—permanent—on carpet,
>   The raveled threads of conversations.

Keys, repeatedly, bending each time at the waist
>   to gather them. Words I knew yesterday.

Boiling pots, dumplings and all. Hardcover books,
>   their covered corners into fleshy tops of feet.

The children of friends.
>   Friends.

II.

Objects in a vacuum fall at the same rate—
>   boulder the same as a feather or mateless sock.

Your body. Mine. If, in a vacuum, my grip gave way,
>   would you drop to the ground with me?

Would we come crashing to the pavement
>   at the same rate, both bruising knees?

We do not live in a vacuum. We swim in a chamber
        pumped with air, with particulate and noise

which slow us, buoy our gobs of matter in deciduous
        rotations: bodies spin, tossed according

to the manner in which air currents hook at planes.
        If you are lucky, with many angles of cellulose,

you fall at the rate of the downy, furred leaf.
        I drop like a bullet shot into mud.

III.

Force attracts us, we two in our bodies.
        If our bags full of guts and nerve contain

all the same space and arrangement of particles,
        our gravity holds each other at the same millionth

of a Newton. But I who am smaller, I who shrink
        —and seemingly daily—spin toward you,

your gravitational pull going to work
        on my lacey bone and thinning skin.

Will you notice the force you exert
        as I collapse into your orbit?

IV.

But gravity moves both ways. It is not simply
        the drag of earth that pulls mass home;

We too heave the earth toward self.
        Shrinking the gap between us and ground,

our movement calls the world forward. We do not
        accelerate alone—the ground itself rises

to catch us. But we are small bodies,
        not intergalactic chunks of rock

hurtling toward a ditch. We'll never notice
        when it happens, that shudder of molecular dust

as the soil itself anticipates a fall, readies
        a spot, just body-sized, in waiting earth.

The ground will rise to gather us all,
        but it catches some of us sooner.

III.
I May Appear Drunk

I May Appear Drunk

When the dog tag arrives by mail,
it is too small. An inch long at best,
the front surface is all but covered
by a medic alert symbol, a staff

twined by two snakes in shadow.
On the back, carved warnings crowd
the metal plate. They leave no margin,
no space around the Latin term

that slurs a diagnosis, each word
brushing the next. It cautions that I
will have trouble breathing. My eyes
will lack focus. I won't form words

that sound like speech. I'll try to stand
and fail. Check my purse for pills, it says,
and for emergency phone numbers.
No room to say the rest, to explain

that where bones anchor my cloudy
film of a soul, I contain mysteries.
I want to say that if my pupils swing
from side to side, they aren't unlike

the eyes of God, pendulous on a thread.
That they're coiled tight in the hum
of the planet's whirling. If I smack my face
to the soil, knocking myself senseless,

then I have learned the ecstasies just
as Saint Theresa knew them, my body
so still you'll never see me rise, never
notice me levitate. My breath crackles

with all Saint Julian learned as paralysis
filched her toes, then knees. What remained
was her knowledge beyond all telling:
we must both fall and be aware of falling.

There aren't enough lines on a pendant
for this. Give me more metal, titanium
to engrave with gaudy serifs and blackfill.
Give me a hammered breastplate, a shield

that molds each rib. Carve in script that
all will be well, and all manner of thing
will be right. Let the steel smoke when I press
a thumb to its surface. Let each word swim

as though in molten lead, pulsing in time
with the earth's black core. Burning emblem,
bonfire heart. Not this tiny caduceus,
this glitter of steel at my breast.

In the Infusion Center,

we appear overnight, odd
numbers scattered about,
looming in manner of toadstools.
Heads furred, stems rooted to chairs,
budgeless. Here comes the nurse
and there the needle,

thereafter the gurney
and curtained room.
Prickle of nerve and bloody meat,
hair popped loose of follicle.
The janitor huffs about our feet,
vacuums up our evidence,

our body bits gone to slag to heap.
Hot grinds the sun on fish tank,
and we note the clownfish and loathe him.
Pretty tail, so sparkly fin, we don't endorse
his peeking orange. Give us the suckerfish,
devourer of the green-grown slime.

"In The Kingdom of Thud, Globes Plummet to Black"

— Madeline Defrees, "Plum Rain"

In the kingdom of thud
the shaking comes and goes.
By three in the afternoon,
I suspect that it will stay.
The pear I'm holding drops
to the linoleum, and I consider
my options. I come down on knees,
creep along linoleum.
I consider the floor's dust.
I am shell-hunched, hunched low,
creeping across my small kingdom
as the shaking comes and goes.
The floor wonders will I stay,
consider the pear, flesh bruised
in three places. Juice rises
to the kingdom of air, of flies,
three of which suckle the pear's meat
as they hunch, stubby legs waving.
Mouths pulse as the juice
goes dripping to the linoleum.
Lifting the pear from the floor's dust,
I am king of the wounded fruit.

Immunosuppressive Therapy: I (a praise song)

Praise the Dettol wipes, and praise
        the four-pack on sale at the megamart.

Praise the clingwrap that holds each tube
        in an inviolable monument to cleanliness.

Praise them for the 99.9 percent
        of viruses and germs that they slaughter

on hard surfaces, and praise the asterisk
        that limits the reader's interpretation

of "germs." Praise the ammonium chloride
        and praise the alkylites, C1 through 12,

for their activity and for their efficacy,
        and praise the unlisted *other ingredients*

that support, that bolster, that aid them
        in their killing. We will not fear the virus

that shudders in a streak of disinfectant,
        or the influenza A2 that drops the limbs

of its protein structure. We place our trust
        the plastic ring of the pull-top can that offers up

its contents, that gives us all we need.
        Praise the counters as they glisten for thirty

minimum seconds, then lay hands upon them.
>Rub your palms across the sticky surfaces.

Touch fingers to your face because
>you can, for nothing will harm you and no fluid

will gather in your lungs. Praise the calluses
>on your fingertips as they inure to chemicals

with your daily ministrations to doorknobs,
>with your semiweekly attention to light switches.

Praise the hours of your life spent swabbing
>at toilet, at faucet, at refrigerator handle.

Celebrate the Dettol wipe by covering floors
>with their soaked, seven-by-eight quadrangles.

Unfurl the wipes and string them as drip-dripping
>banners at the door's lintel. Let them anoint

all who enter your doors, all who bring you gifts
>carried in the secret places beneath fingernails.

Pray that they will not fail you or forsake you
>against the hard-running noses of winter children.

Immunosuppressive Therapy II (a litany)

Start at the beginning:
                               from the stranger
sneezing into her hand on the Underground,
her palm blessing the metal handrail
before hallowing the top of each seat
in a stumble-step through the driver's
hard brake.
                           Or the toothless baby
gum-gumming a metal shopping cart,
bubbling a spittle-glaze on cool steel.

You know what follows.
                           That dullest of heat
that rises through the scalp, each pore
a damp constellation that slicks the hair
in a fever sweat. The throat blazes itself tight,
wants for water. Tender flesh between ribs
plumps with each muscle-flailing cough.
Go to bed. Repeat tomorrow. Weeks pass.

Begin again:
                        Streptococcus pneumoniae
lives in throat even on good days,
and a sharp breath alone is enough to pluck
it free of the tonsil, force it through alveoli,
nest it inside the lung. The colony itself,
pillowed and light as a fluff of cotton, looks
kindly enough. But it doesn't mind
taking advantage of raw tissue.
It doesn't ask if you'd like to let it in.

Start the antibiotics.
                                 The X-rays show
small pools within the lung, puddles insistent
as snow melt. Bacteria gather, swaddle the ribs
with cloudy down, and all your fevered wishing
for breath warms the snow bank further,
heats the drift, pools the water, dampens
your every inward heave for air. Amoxicillin
stirs in your bloodstream, works itself heartward.

Begin again.
                                 Feel yourself as the rat at the gate
of its cardboard maze. Take the train downtown.
Breathe deep, cough hard. Separate cartilage
from bone and muscle at the sternum. View
the white of your bone on film. Take X-Ray slides
again. Watch the fluid pocket in your lung. Take
the amoxicillin. Begin again. Take the train.

Immunosuppressive Therapy: III (a prayer)

Let the student who has chosen to sit before me
suffer from nothing but allergies. Let his sneezes
reach nowhere but the crook of his own elbow.

Let the pulp fibers of turned-in essays harbor no
virus, and let the suspect blobs that speckle
the table's surface be nothing more than motes of dust,

not remnants of lunch with colonies-in-sauce.
Let the teacher who last touched this whiteboard pen
have washed his hands sometime today, and let

the thermostat with its teeming knobs need no
adjustments for these two hours of lecture. Let
the girl who never brings a pencil to this class

have no need to borrow mine, but let her neighbor
do unto her as he would have her do unto him
and lend a biro from the secret pouch of his bag.

Let the coffee I have drunk be long in its coursing
within me, for the bathroom is out of soap again.
The toilet paper, too, has pared away to strips

of glue on cardboard roll. Let me be spared
the touching of the classroom's doorknob,
for I have watched a student cough into his palm,

then lay hold of the handle with juicy touch.
Let me manage the semblance of lucid speech
as I hold forth about the proper use of semicolons,

for my mind is otherwise arrested by the a wad
of tissue on carpet that hasn't been vacuumed
since 1992. Let me breathe as little as possible,

but for what air I do need, let the heater ducts
be free of mold and spore, as the hand sanitizer
stings itself into the cracked skin of knuckles.

"Doctors baffled about why H1N1 targets young, healthy"
— *Global News*, Canada

The flu season comes in its usual tide
of cough syrup, cherry reds and arsenic
green. Kleenex bunts the couches
of waiting rooms, drapes the desktops

in offices. News headlines pump hysteria
across the wire, make a virus's replication
into a particular insult to *healthy adults
and children.* Pictures show lines at clinics:

men with shirtsleeves rolled up, injection sites
bared with high gravity. The hordes look
like a pitiful regiment, ready to march to war
against viruses that threaten the American Way.

Experts appear from clavicle up,
their televised jaws slack-flapping the same
blather as always, telling us that usually it's *only
those who have underlying conditions*

who die of influenza. Only us, only the few
shadowy figures barely worth mentioning.
We few, the cancer-bald. Just us, the asthmatics.
Nobody in the death-ranks but we of genetic

mutations. But when film cuts to an image
of a sweat-glazed toddler hooked to electrodes,
It's only we who have *underlying conditions*
who know how to say, *Oh, baby, little one, I know.*

Immunosuppressive Therapy: IV
(as suspense film)

They're synthetic adrenaline,
        these pale, scored pills—
        little grenades of false stress

telling the heart to muscle
        faster, to slap its chambers
and ready the host for battle.

        Every nerve ending
vibrates with the smallest draft,
scorches with the brush

        of wool fiber on skin.
        Pores blossom, open to sweat
in oily buds, and eardrums beat

a ragged tattoo even when the body
is still. The feeling is not unlike
        suspense: the gut-throb,

        the eye-squint,
the *tell-me-when-it's-over* posture
           of the audience

at a horror movie screening.
        Background music thrums,
        and the on-screen ingénue

hesitates at a door we don't
        want her to enter.   *Don't open it—*
but that door may as well

be the microwave's hatch
        or cupboard's hinge,
the free-swinging porthole

        of washing machine
or mailbox: none are any different:
        what lurks behind each one

          whether spider
          whether dust mote
takes on that theatrical glow

        of panic, the day's tasks sing
to a soundtrack of   *Don't open it—*
        of   *check around the corner,*

of *somebody's watching me*
        as I key open the door,
          cross the threshold

          of my own house,
    I stand, frozen to listen
          as though for a rustle

from some unseemly corner of closet.
          I hear only the tempo
of my hard-running heart,

sense only the needle-point prickle of hair
        standing at the base of my neck.
As I dig in my purse for an evening dose,

I push the prescription bottle's cap,
          and the music looms
in a distant minor key.

Don't open it—

Round for Corticosteroids

Always willing to sit down, lie down, lie flatter, etc. But I am taking
cortisone so I will have to get up again.
— Flannery O'Connor, letter to Betty Boyd Love, 1950

The alarm pings for the next dose of cortisone,
and the pill bottle rattles excitement.
Tongue to stomach, pills fight to crawl back up,
and the high-pressure blood-nozzle
drums behind the brain. Next, the fever,
the shedding of clothes, the pink skin in winter,
every fat pore mewling with sweat.
The pill bottle rattles excitement.

Hard-heaving blood drums in the brain,
butters itself on the skull's interior.
The alarm is screwed tight for the next dose.
Next, the fever, while high-pressure blood
goes drum-beating down the brain.
The stomach rock-tumbles each pill that fights
to crawl its way up, bleeds and protests with twists
that will be calmed by no milk and no cracker.

The bloody heart keeps clapping, and pink skin
with its fat pores sings a chorus in time.
The skull's interior drags, fatty as butter,
as the pill bottle rattles excitement.
The nozzle sets loose the fever
as the stomach twits in protest, begs the body
to sit down, lie down, lie flatter, until
ping—the alarm demands the next dose.

Intravenous Immunoglobulin Therapy: I

Intravenous immunoglobulin is a blood product prepared from the serum of between 1,000 and 15,000 donors per batch. It is the treatment of choice for patients with antibody deficiencies.
— US National Library of Medicine

The neurologist says I'm *like one of those people who'd rather saw off an arm*

than give a speech in public. I have to agree:
it's similar, this bleak terror of needles

that makes me curl on myself,
crab-hooking my arms at the mention

of *infusion.* I remind him of the scene
I caused last time he waved me upstairs

to the lab. Sweaty fainter, I hit the floor
as soon as the rubber lasso cracked free

at the end of a basic blood draw.
My current acquaintance with linoleum floor

(and with laces of fellow patients' shoes)
suffices me. Still, he orders it,

this days-long infusion with a cocktail
of donor cells. The plasma

from an army of others, refined and pooled
to thin my own, wayward blood.

A few hours each time, a few times each week—
I drop my head between my knees,

ready to faint before we've begun.
If we hit you with enough valium, he says,

you won't care about the needle.
I know he's right, imagine myself lolled

in a head slump as the nurses prod for veins.
But how to explain the rest of it: the knowledge

of those legions marching through the private
reaches of the body? And how to think with the hundred

strangers creeping through the capillaries
of my brain? To contain an embarrassed blush

for a crowd? To chew a knob of bread
when I teem with a thousand others' absent teeth?

Intravenous Immunoglobulin Therapy: II

This isn't what Whitman meant when he said
I contain multitudes. He wasn't talking about
this slow emptying of plasma from sealed bag

to bloodstream. The thousand therapeutic flecks
of other bodies, other DNA plumping my veins
until they rise from my skin in a triumphal shade

of blue. It's not what he had in mind, yet I also
feel too full and contradict myself; despite
having called the insurance line twice each day

for a month to secure my spot in this darkened room,
I eye the *EXIT*. I estimate the number of strides
to the elevator, plot how to slip past blonde nurse Mary

if only I could slide from the infusion chair
with its piled and voluminous cushion.
The IV port itself is a queasy business, the way

it rides for inches up the vein, spreading cold
and stinging plumes across the arm, the phantom
taste of metal buttering my tongue. But it's the drip

of the faceless army that makes me want to run,
that stirs a primal desire to flee. If, on the street,
someone tried to claw beneath my layers of skin,

to wash though my brain and blink out from my two
startled eyes, I could have him arrested, blast him
senseless with pepper spray. But anonymous

in a plastic bag, they come for me by thousands,
a phalanx knocking the inside of my skull.
And I am meant to sit, let them march me over

as I sit, motionless, in the dark. Each click
of the infusion pump makes me want to zip
its sticky dressing free, to pull the failing line

from my burning vein. But there's no shelter
from this friendly invasion. The multitudes have drawn
a tactical map in my veins, claimed my body for their own.

Etymological Note

Before the seventeenth century,
the English language had no noun
for *comfort*. No way to describe

that state of better-off-ness
for sleeping on a bed of hay
than on a bare plank. No word

to express how much that hay's
texture might be improved
without the creep of insect

or midnight scuttle of mouse.
Comfort was only a verb—to solace,
to strengthen, to give what aid

or blessing one could against
a hemorrhagic wound or lung
splitting with rot. To be

comfortable meant nothing beyond
able to bear someone else's idea
of help: the smoke of censer

at prayer, the crumbling wafer
of last rites—bodily gestures
that lead a spirit into the dark.

When the nurse cracks the door,
the thin wedge of light raking
at my eyes, reminding my body

that it is body still, she asks if I
am comfortable. I say yes, reach out
my silent hand for touch.

IV.
The Unreal Woman, Post-Operative

The Unreal Woman, Post-Operative

I.

Sound reaches me first
        on the fading current

of anesthesia, light finding me
        long after the rattle

        of IV pump, alarm bells
                on oximeters,

and the voice an elderly man
        who shouts down the inches
between our beds

as though surgeons
        were cutting him still.
                At first, I can't parse them,

        his monosyllables that rise and burst
in the air between us.

I worry for a moment about purgatory.

        I hear a nurse ask the man
if he's feeling too much pain. *No*, he says,
        I need someone to cut my toenails.

And through my bruised windpipe
        where the ventilator's newly gone,
                I laugh, or try to laugh but wheeze,

and the overhead bulbs
            spread a bright wash
                        across my closed eyelids.

I feel my mind slip into that self-on-a-gurney,

            sweaty and incised, prone on a sheet.
I rub my dry and splitting lips together and think

*what I wouldn't give
        for a tube of lip balm.*

My body too has its comedic and mewling demands.

II.

Three incisions on each side of the chest—
that's what the surgeon said I could expect.

I imagined they'd look like buttonholes
sewn shut, neat and geometrically spaced

in the valleys between my ribs. What he didn't say
was that each split in the skin

would be irregular, shaped only like itself
and set into the chest like buckshot,

a visually random assault. And no one mentioned
the rough slice into breasts, that most tender

fat, or the tunneling through their mass.
There wasn't any pamphlet for this, no mention

of the fact that, where muscle is sliced through,
so too are nerves, and where they leave

their severed ends, they spark and crackle
like powerlines downed in a storm,

lighting up the shape of what's been pared away.
Except, of course, for where neurons

have been butchered too much to return,
have abandoned their project of feeling. No pain,

yet no sensation at all. A flat and expressionless flesh.
This wasn't written in any patient's guide—

how to contain the firework crackle
in the dead expanse over my heart.

III.

If the blood pressure cuff
didn't boa-constrict every
fifteen minutes, and if
the fluorescent lights
overhead would dim.
If the man haunting the hall
would stop the monologues
on real estate that he delivers
into his clamshell phone
as his grandmother wheezes
in the next room over. If
the arterial line would quit
staring up like an eerie little eye

in a silent threat to bleed me out
with every bend of the wrist.
If incisions didn't sear at a twitch
of muscle. If the morphine
in the IV pump would not
sputter out for the hour. If it weren't
for this incessant buzz of fly,
its beating of wing on window—

IV.

Live from the surgical ward,
it's a nonstop performance,

        a can-can dance
                with medication cups,
        a soft-shoe shift change
                of nurses all night.

Somewhere down the hall, a speaker
honks out *Mary Had a Little Lamb*,

        and orderlies fleet-foot through halls
        to those air-horn tones that signify
                nothing good.

Cindy the Heparin Nurse strolls in, jazz-hands
a fan of quick-retract needles. Show her
        your abdominal fat
            if you have any.

Get the hot, blood-thinning sting
        over with for a four-hour stretch.

A supporting cast of respiratory therapists
        grapevines in with props,
                forever impatient, forever
                holding plentiful devices
                with mysterious valves
                                and gauges.
        Don't you know the drill by now?

They won't explain to you
        how you must latch on and puff, latch on

and heave, latch on and huffle-snort
        into plastic that smells like a kiddie pool.

You are meant to know.
You are meant to unspeakingly
play your role.

They scribble notes as to your performance
promise—or threaten—to return.

                And all the while, the roller derby
                of patients in sticky-tread socks
                goes looping down the corridor.

                The man with the scalp stuck full
                of electrodes takes first position,
                then the man you know as Burt,

                        Burt who on each lap stops to say
                        God bless you, friend, Burt
                        canes his way to a close second.

But you, with your IV pole and its several
plump and swinging bags, your pop-a-wheelie
oxygen tank, your chest tube pump that demands

to be carried like a little briefcase of blood,
                          you're at a distinct

                          disadvantage. The other patients lap you
                          and lap you in their Jell-O fuelled
          rumble,
                          their hip-checking battle of speed.

You waddle as if at the center ring as the circus—
the whole reeling wheel of it—rotates around you,

the wheels of tank and pole squeak to announce you,
your set of pale buttocks in a flapping-wide gown

          jiggling, a spectacle under the bigtop.

V.

And everywhere the *EXIT* signs point red and flickering,
suggesting that, somewhere, there's a way out.

VI.

On discharge day, a woman
who could be my grandmother
wheels me down the ward,
and I'm tempted to tell her *no,*

to rise from my standard-issue chair
that's two sizes too big and walk.
But swaddled in gauze—like Jesus
half-resurrected—I can't flop

my feet loose, much less waddle
the length of the corridor, navigate
the echoing pit of the parking garage.
Even to crank loose my jaw for speech

requires a focus I can't maintain.
I let my head loll in its opiate droop,
and look to my lap. I note that I
have put my sweats on inside out,

but can't work up enough spirit to blush.
An indignity, yes, but minor, after scores
of personnel have witnessed my bare and pasty
jiggle. And I don't want to ask to stop,

to right my wrong-leggedness for fear
that a nurse, an assistant, an orderly,
an X-ray wielder, a lab tech, a janitor,
a respiratory therapist, a chaplain

will bar my way, demand *one last thing*
before I go. Silently, I urge her on,
this surrogate grandmother of mine.
She bullfrogs *excuse us* and gains

a running clip, plowing my chair
through crowds in the main-floor lobby,
confused delivery men with flowers
and directionless visitors scattering

in our wake. She swings me wide,
backs me into the elevator
that blasts us forth into the muggy
air of the garage. I can taste the exhaust,

the promise of city streets beyond.
I peer behind us, feel certain that someone's
giving chase, declaring that there's been
a mistake. She shoves me free of the chair

and I lunge for the car, fall to my seat,
beg my getaway driver to *go, go faster*
as we churn up the ramp toward daylight.
I fling money at the garage attendant, demand

that he throw wide the gate. And in the searing
mid-day July, we pull onto the avenue,
where ours becomes a single car, any sedan,
any black and scuttling insect

among legions. Nothing to see here,
and nothing special about it,
And I am not a patient to be tracked down
or eyeballed. And the city bus won't spit forth

a team of doctors, their white coats flapping.
And the girl at the crosswalk doesn't want
a laboratory specimen from me. All the man
with his bent cardboard sign demands

is a healthy tribute of change.
And he will not cut me. I will not
be sawed open, and no needle will pierce
the tender ditch of my elbow.

I will drive into the improbable glare
of noontime sun, and I will crank the window
open, let the hot air bathe my arms as we speed
through an endless succession of lights,

green

       after green

              after green—

Acknowledgements

I'm grateful to the editors of the following journals, anthologies, and newspapers for giving many of these poems their first homes:

The Burden of Light, Dialogist, Easy Street Magazine, Gargoyle Magazine, The Los Angeles Review, Moon City Review, Poetry Northwest, The Rumpus, Southern Indiana Review, TYPO, South Carolina Review, and *The New York Times.*

Lightning Source UK Ltd.
Milton Keynes UK
UKHW010112100123
415068UK00007B/823

9 781915 079893